I Am Helpful

By Errol Goodman

 Gareth Stevens
Publishing

Please visit our Web site, www.garethstevens.com. For a free color catalog of all our high-quality books, call toll free 1-800-542-2595 or fax 1-877-542-2596.

Library of Congress Cataloging-in-Publication Data

Goodman, Errol.
I am helpful / Errol Goodman.
   p. cm. – (Kids of character)
Includes index.
ISBN 978-1-4339-4857-2 (pbk.)
ISBN 978-1-4339-4858-9 (6-pack)
ISBN 978-1-4339-4856-5 (library binding)
1. Helping behavior in children–Juvenile literature. 2. Children–Conduct of life–Juvenile literature. I. Title.
BF723.H45G66 2011
179'.9–dc22

                         2010034637

First Edition

Published in 2011 by
Gareth Stevens Publishing
111 East 14th Street, Suite 349
New York, NY 10003

Copyright © 2011 Gareth Stevens Publishing

Editor: Mary Ann Hoffman
Designer: Christopher Logan

Photo credits: Cover, pp. 5, 7, 21 Shutterstock.com; p. 1 Comstock/Thinkstock; p. 9 Jupiterimages/Creatas/Thinkstock; p. 11 Jupiterimages/Pixland/Thinkstock; p. 13 Stockbyte/Thinkstock; p. 15 iStockphoto.com; p. 17 Beto Hacker/Getty Images; p. 19 Jupiterimages/Comstock/Thinkstock.

Printed in the United States of America

CPSIA compliance information: Batch #CW11GS: For further information contact Gareth Stevens, New York, New York at 1-800-542-2595.

Table of Contents

Boldface words appear in the glossary.

Being Helpful

A helpful person does things that need to be done. They are friendly and kind. A helpful person does things for people who cannot do things for themselves.

In the Neighborhood

Bill helps keep his neighborhood looking nice. Every Saturday, Bill and his parents go to the neighborhood park. They pick weeds. They plant flowers. Bill is helpful.

Some people do not have enough to eat. They do not have money to buy food. Ben goes with his family to the **food bank**. He gives food to people who need it. Ben is helpful.

DONATE

FOOD
DRIVE

Ted is Tara's friend. Tara's mother broke her arm. Tara and her mother needed to buy things at the store. Ted walked to the store with them. He helped them get the things they needed. Ted is helpful.

At School

Jack cleaned out his desk. He threw his old papers into the **recycle** bin. There were papers on the floor. Jack picked them up. He threw them into the bin, too. Jack is helpful.

The children were playing. Gina's friend was sad. One of her **favorite** earrings had come off. Gina stopped playing. She helped her friend look for the lost earring. Gina is helpful.

At Home

Sue's mother goes to work every day. She is tired when she gets home. Each night after dinner, Sue washes the dirty dishes. Sue is helpful.

Bob's mother and father were busy inside the house. They asked Bob to watch his sister. Bob took his sister into the yard. He played games with her. Bob is helpful.

Nina's family has a pet dog. Nina walks the dog every day. She feeds the dog, too. Nina is helpful.

Glossary

favorite: the most liked

food bank: a place that has food for people in need

recycle: to be used again

For More Information

Books

Berry, Joy. *Let's Talk About Being Helpful.* New York, NY: Joy Berry Enterprises, 2008.

Mayer, Cassie. *Being Helpful.* Chicago, IL: Heinemann Library, 2008.

Web Sites

YouthSITE
www.servicelearning.org/youthsite/k-5
Learn ways to help your community.

Kelly Bear Behavior
www.kellybear.com/ActivityBehavior.html
Read and discuss phrases that can help you know what good behavior is.

Index